STORMS IN OUR LIVES

Inspirational Stories for Soldiers and Their Families

Colonel Tom Greco, USA (Retired)

Storms in Our Lives
Inspirational Stories for Soldiers and Their Families
By Tom Greco
Aloha Publishing © 2023

Aloha Publishing supports copyright. Copyright fuels creativity, encourages diverse voices, promotes free speech, and creates a vibrant culture. Thank you for buying an authorized edition of this book and for complying with copyright laws by not reproducing, scanning, or distributing any part of it in any form without permission.

While the publisher and author have used their best efforts in preparing this book, they make no representations or warranties with respect to the accuracy or completeness of this book and specifically disclaim any implied warranties of merchantability or fitness for a particular purpose. No warranty may be created or extended by sales representatives or written sales materials. The advice and strategies contained herein may not be suitable for your situation. You should consult a professional where appropriate. The stories and interviews in this book are true although the names and identifiable information may have been changed to maintain confidentiality.

The publisher and author shall have neither liability nor responsibility to any person or entity with respect to loss, damage, or injury caused or alleged to be caused directly or indirectly by the information contained in this book. The information presented herein is in no way intended as a substitute for counseling or other professional guidance.

All Bible verses are from the English Standard Version (ESV) unless otherwise stated.

Print ISBN: 978-1-61206-295-2
eBook ISBN: 978-1-61206-296-9

Published by Aloha Publishing

Printed in the United States of America

Dedication

To Gail, for your incredible and steadfast love over the years. Words are inadequate to express my love for you. No matter how many years pass by in our marriage, there will always be two moments when I want to be with you—now and forever!

To General David A. Bramlett, my commander, mentor, coach, and wonderful friend. You molded me into the Army officer, husband, father, and grandfather I am today. Thank you for investing in me.

To the incredibly brave and extremely competent officers and soldiers of Task Force 3-187 Infantry in the 101st Airborne Division (Air Assault). Thank you for the privilege of being your commander in peace and war. Your courage, competence, commitment, and integrity were inspiring and continue to challenge me every day. Rakkasan!

Contents

How to Engage With This Book	7
Introduction: The Storm in My Life	11
Day 1: Courage	21
Day 2: Safety and Refuge	25
Day 3: Giants	30
Day 4: Ranger Buddy	34
Day 5: The Power to Choose	38
Day 6: Signal Mirrors	42
Day 7: Death Zone	46
Day 8: A Cup of Decaf	50
Day 9: Adversity	54
Day 10: Anchored	58
Day 11: Civic Virtue	62
Day 12: A Gentle Answer	66
Day 13: Consistency is Key	70
Day 14: Worth	74
Day 15: My Banner is Clear	79
Day 16: Less Bark, More Wag	83
Day 17: Never Quit	87

Day 18: Always There	91
Day 19: A Road Not Taken	94
Day 20: Enough	98
Day 21: Limitations	102
Day 22: Fear is a Liar	106
Day 23: Recovery	110
Day 24: Rest	114
Day 25: Success	118
Day 26: Two by Two	122
Day 27: Trophies	127
Day 28: Wisdom	131
Day 29: Trust and Humility	135
Day 30: Waiting	138
Day 31: Hope in God	141
Final Thoughts	145
Acknowledgments	149
About the Author	151

How to Engage With This Book

Soldiers and their families are a special gift to our nation. Their sacrifice, diligence, commitment, and love of country and each other are unlike any group of citizens in our nation.

I am also well aware that many soldiers struggle with faith issues when confronted with the horrors of combat, the loneliness and oftentimes long separation from their families and friends, and the real and present possibility of losing their lives on the battlefield. I decided to focus this book on messages that articulate important spiritual concepts for soldiers and their families.

As I prayed and read His Word, I saw how Jesus used parables to share truth and wisdom with His disciples and the many crowds who listened to Him during His ministry on Earth.

Jesus bypassed the religious leaders and took His message straight to the people. He understood He had to communicate in a way that would resonate with them. Jesus knew people become more engaged when they listen to a story. Engaging each person who listened with common, everyday events allowed Jesus's teachings to hit home and helped His listeners remember and share these truths with others.

Frequently, spiritual discussions revolve around abstract concepts. Due to this perceived complexity, many soldiers avoid them as impractical or unhelpful. Sometimes they simply cannot wrap their heads around the ideas of grace, forgiveness, and surrendering to God. They simply cannot see the connection between these concepts and how to live their lives today. I also understand the power and dynamics of a war story, often shared with those we have been privileged to lead, both in peace and combat.

In this book, you will read stories that connect Biblical truth with my real-life experiences as a soldier and leader. Trying to follow the model that Jesus used, I offer a Biblical passage and share a personal experience, a soldier insight, or a life lesson that connects to what was written in the Bible, the Word of God. At the end of each story, I offer you an action, idea, or question to engage with to help reinforce the lesson.

I encourage you to make time each day to read one devotional. Perhaps open your Bible or go online and read the verse—better yet, the entire chapter— to better understand the context in which the story was written. As you read my stories, read with your eyes and listen with your heart.

My prayer is that you can connect events in your own life to those reflected in the stories. I trust the Holy Spirit will help you move in the right direction and take the appropriate action.

If you are a parent, grandparent, relative, or friend of a soldier or military family, please consider sharing this book with them. Perhaps share a story that touched your heart or that speaks to a situation your soldier or military family recently encountered. You can also give this book as a gift before the soldier leaves on a deployment.

I hope you enjoy these stories and will take this book as an invitation to better learn who Jesus Christ is and how much He loves you.

You are loved,
T. Greco
Star, Idaho

INTRODUCTION

The Storm in My Life

I commanded an air assault infantry task force in the 101st Airborne Division. Our unit was designed to move throughout the battlefield by helicopters. Our unique mobility and ability to quickly mass forces on a target were critical to our success. As the commander, our nation and Army entrusted me with the lives and mission accomplishment of this 1,500-soldier force. During Desert Storm, our unit was selected to helicopter assault deep behind Iraqi lines to seize and secure critical positions along a strategic highway. We were to deny the Iraqi forces the ability to reinforce or retreat. It was a highly complex air assault forced entry operation.

To accomplish this mission, our task force would be air assaulted deep into enemy territory, only 125 miles from Baghdad. We were to be the most northern allied coalition force in Iraq, and our task force was to be isolated from any other U.S. or allied force. When we would fight, we would have to be prepared to fight in all directions. When I received this mission, a senior officer told me our anticipated casualty rate for this insertion could be very high.

Several weeks before this forced entry into Iraq, we had been conducting extensive rehearsals for our mission. Being a West Point graduate and having many critical assignments during my then 19 years of service, I felt that I was highly skilled in the art of modern warfare. Deep inside, however, I had this feeling that I was going at it all wrong. Pride, conceit, arrogance, and confidence in myself had consumed me. In retrospect, I acted like I did not need God. Time and time again, my plans and our rehearsal efforts were abysmal and constantly thwarted by various events, which in hindsight were clearly the Lord's way of telling me to trust in Him, not in myself. Proverbs 3:5 reminds us to trust in the Lord and not lean on our own understanding.

One evening before I retired for the night, I read about Joshua's experiences in trusting God at the battle of Jericho. Inexplicably, I felt the Lord's presence in my tent. I realized at that moment that I was not giving this battle to the Lord. It was as if the Lord spoke directly to my heart. I broke down and cried. I had let the Lord down in so many ways. Fear of losing my soldiers' lives because of my stupidity and arrogance gripped me. My heart actually ached. On my knees, crying, I first praised God and then asked the Lord for forgiveness.

Continuing in prayer, I surrendered to Him. I asked Him to lead my task force, to take us into battle to do His will, and that our efforts would truly glorify

Him. I told Him the battle was His; I was His servant, and I fully trusted Him. At that moment, a calm and peace I had never before experienced engulfed me. My tears stopped. The pain in my chest quickly abated. I knew God was now my leader on this mission. I was absolutely confident that I, like Paul writes to the Philippians, could "do all things through Him who strengthens me."

The next days before the combat air assault were a blur. We continued with training and rehearsals, but there was something different in our soldiers and in me. My soldiers could not explain it, but they noticed I was different. Our rehearsals also went from poor execution to operational excellence.

Finally, in the early morning of February 24th, our time had come. His time had come! Our satellite and reconnaissance planes told us we could be flying between and behind elements of two Iraqi divisions, which contained 5,000-6,000 soldiers each. These enemy troops were also equipped with the latest Soviet-made equipment, including surface-to-air hand-held missiles. On top of all that, the weather was cold and rainy.

Our UH-60 Blackhawk helicopters, loaded with 14 heavy-laden soldiers, would be flying 150 miles deep into Iraq less than 15 feet off the ground at 90-100 miles per hour, with the pilots wearing night vision goggles. Our vehicles and artillery would follow in

CH-47 Chinook support helicopters, and because of the Chinook's fuel limitations, these aircraft would have to land 60 miles short of our objective and drive cross-country to link up with the remainder of our forces. To compound this complex scheme, the Euphrates River had recently flooded and made the area extremely muddy and often impassable in places. There were also no roads to speak of.

Just before we launched our first helicopter sorties, an unexpected storm appeared. We had a very limited window of opportunity to fly our forces into the objective area, and this storm threatened to push us out of this window. It appeared we might have to conduct this assault in daylight instead of under the cover of darkness. All of this added to the danger of being seen and acquired by the enemy's sophisticated air defense weaponry. The storm brought in a fog that was so thick I could not see my hand in front of my face. I knew we could not immediately and safely fly in this weather. The storm continued, pushing us into a high-risk daylight lift-off. From 3 a.m. until 8 a.m., we waited in desperate anticipation for the weather to clear.

The fog finally lifted at 8:45 a.m. Our first sorties flew into Iraq at 9 a.m. in clear daylight. Every helicopter flew perfectly. Each one landed right on target. We had enemy contact on landing, but they quickly scattered, ran away, or were killed. Our vehicles and artillery quickly followed us to their appointed landing zones

60 miles behind us. They landed without incident and began the trek to link up with us. A sandstorm that occurred in the morning had put a sandy coating on the muddy fields and created what looked and felt like a road. This allowed our vehicles to travel at 60 miles per hour or better.

Later that day I also found out there were two other storms, one on the left and one on the right of our line of flight. It was as if the storm we had experienced in the early morning hours moved ahead of us and then moved to the left and right of our flight path. God created a corridor for us to fly into Iraq and prevented any of the Iraqis on our flanks from visually acquiring us.

Our soldiers advanced to their assigned objectives. The flooding had been more extensive than our photos showed. We could not dig foxholes because of the high water table. We also did not want to build up our positions, thus telling the Iraqis, "Here we are." We conceded that to maintain our position, we would have to remain exposed, both to the elements and the enemy.

Intense fighting occurred within hours of our landing. Several Iraqi units tried to penetrate our positions. The air was streaked with red tracer fire. The sound and crash of mortar and artillery fire and explosions were deafening. At times we fought enemy units trying to break through our positions from the north, south, and west simultaneously.

On Day Two, the weather had soured again; cloud cover and dense fog came in, and our soldiers were cold, wet, and scared. Our USAF air cover and attack helicopter support were unable to support us. We were alone on the battlefield, sitting ducks for the Iraqi artillery and tanks. We had no cover from artillery, no place to hide, no air support, and no way, except by foot, to run or evacuate any wounded. But we had, in our hearts, in my heart, God's promise that He was our leader.

Late that night, we received word that our intelligence found out that Iraqi Republican Guard armor brigade was coming north to push us off the highway. They were one of Iraq's most elite forces, and our soldiers had nowhere to hide.

For the next two days, we fought violent fights. The landscape around our positions was surreal. Burning vehicles littered the fields. Large craters from artillery were everywhere, and numerous Iraqis lay dead on the roads and fields around us. The fields smelled like death. We waited for the Iraqi brigade to come, but it never did attack us. The initial report I received was that this Iraqi brigade just disappeared from any radar.

We later found out the Iraqi armor brigade that was advancing toward our positions was stalled by bad weather, sandstorms, and poor roads. This Iraqi brigade was decimated by another Army mechanized/tank unit as the storm lifted in the early morning of Day Three. The two parallel storms on Day One and the storm on Days Two and Three often remind me of the events and God's provision during the exodus of the Israeli nation from Egypt.

The cease-fire order came on Day Four. The coalition forces, more than 400 miles south of us, had defeated the Iraqi forces and liberated Kuwait. The war was over just four days later. On the day of the cease-fire, I gave orders to our leaders to maintain security and allow our soldiers to get some much-needed sleep. I requested a resupply of ammunition and hot meals for our soldiers as my staff prepared for our next mission. I also asked my commanders for a situation report. We had killed or captured hundreds of Iraqis and destroyed scores of vehicles, but none of our soldiers were wounded or killed. Not one soldier even had a scratch!

Afterward, I found a small irrigation pump shed and sat down beside it. The emotions of the past four days overwhelmed me. I cried tears of joy. I realized God was truly our leader in this fight. He heard and answered my prayer. There was no way our force could have survived and won this fight without Him being in absolute control. What we experienced was not luck or chance. As my chaplain later said, "It was a God thing." At that moment, I dedicated my life to Jesus. I told Him I would go wherever He led me and would do His will, wherever and whenever He called. I would serve Him and be His servant for the rest of my life.

To this day, I have attempted to keep this promise and my faith in Him. I continue to serve our Lord, be unafraid to speak the Gospel, be bold for Christ in all situations, live my life in as Christ-like a manner as I can, and tell the story of my turning point. I want to join Jesus in His work—wherever He assigns me. I simply want to join Him because I love Him.

I also want others to experience the peace and calm I found in Him in that tent and on the battlefield. I want others to know that despite the storms in their lives, God is able, God is consistent, God loves, and God cares. He is only a prayer away.

We all face Desert Storms in our lives. These Desert Storms are sometimes far more dramatic and much more personal than my story. Maybe you are dealing with a Desert Storm disguised as a bad report from your doctor, finding a meaningful job, financial issues, recovering from a bad relationship, dependence on alcohol or drugs, your marriage is on the ropes, your teenage child's behavior is frightful, or whatever.

After reading my testimony, if you feel God is calling you to join Him, if you desire God to forgive you, if you want God to be the leader of your life—to give Him your fears and to trust in Him from today until you are with Him for eternity—I encourage you to simply invite Him into your heart right now.

If you want to talk or pray together, email me at stormsinourlives@gmail.com, and I promise to try to connect within 24 hours.

You are loved,
Tom

DAY 1

Courage

"Be strong and courageous, for you shall cause this people to inherit the land that I swore to their fathers to give them. Only be strong and very courageous, being careful to do according to all the law that Moses my servant commanded you. Do not turn from it to the right hand or to the left, that you may have good success wherever you go. This Book of the Law shall not depart from your mouth, but you shall meditate on it day and night, so that you may be careful to do according to all that is written in it. For then you will make your way prosperous, and then you will have good success. Have I not commanded you? Be strong and courageous. Do not be frightened, and do not be dismayed, for the Lord your God is with you wherever you go." Joshua 1:6-9

When Moses died, God appointed Joshua to lead the nation of Israel into the Promised Land. Have you ever taken over a position from someone else? Perhaps it was a family business or a farm from a parent or relative? Ever replace a retiring teacher, nurse, or successful manager? Ever taken over a key leadership position from another leader in your unit, in a club, committee, or elected office? Maybe you took over from another coach?

I remember when I was an Army Captain. I was selected to be a battalion operations officer ahead of several very senior officers who outranked me, had served many more years of service, and had combat service in Vietnam. Talk about pressure. I felt like if I blew it just one time, those senior officers would be hunting for my head and demanding my firing.

Now think about Joshua. Moses was the only leader the nation of Israel knew for over 40 years. Moses spoke to God and God spoke to Moses. Moses, with God as his helper, performed miracles in front of their eyes. Then suddenly, Joshua was calling all the shots. He had to coordinate the movement of thousands of people. He had to ensure they had food and water. He had to lead them into battle, fight an entrenched enemy, and win. Any loss, misstep, or strategic or operational failure could be death to his nation.

Like a coach before the game or the leader of a night attack, Joshua's life was pressure-packed. I believe Joshua was really wondering if he was the right guy for this position. Did he have what it took to fulfill his duties in this position? Could he meet this challenge?

God gave Joshua assurance that he was ready. With the words from God's own mouth, Joshua realized he had what it took to get through this challenge. He had God.

While we might not be in a crucial leadership role right now, we do face challenges every day. I can say with great confidence that our lives are pressure-packed, whether it's losing a job, finding that money is tight, or worrying about the next deployment.

Now for the Joshua question: Do you have what it takes to get through these challenging times? To get through this time of unemployment, financial calamity, loneliness, or illness? To make it through this fear of the unknown?

I believe with all my heart that if we rely on God and trust Him with everything we have, the answer to all of these questions is *yes!* He has commanded us to be strong and courageous. That's what He wants us to be.

ENGAGE

What challenges are you facing today? Do you question if you are the right person to lead your family, your team, or your unit right now?

Write down the challenges that you are facing. After you have done that, offer each one up to God in prayer, trusting Him to give you the courage and wisdom to overcome them.

DAY 2

Safety and Refuge

"Whoever dwells in the shelter of the Most High will rest in the shadow of the Almighty. I will say of the Lord, 'He is my refuge and my fortress, my God, in whom I trust.'" Psalm 91:1-2 NIV

A week ago, I spoke to a homeless veteran in his early 30s and invited him to have a sandwich and coffee with me at a local coffee shop. He openly shared with me his traumatic childhood, abusive father, alcoholic mother, and his in-and-out journey with foster care. When he graduated from high school, he joined the Army.

After seeing two of his friends being blown up in Afghanistan, he chose not to reenlist. He tried construction for a while and said he did quite well until he got hurt on a roofing job and landed in the hospital for seven weeks. During his recovery, he was prescribed pain-killing drugs, and after he was discharged, he still had leg and back pain and could not work for several months. During this lull, he found peace living on the streets and asking for handouts to buy more painkillers.

He shared a lesson he learned from his youth that was confirmed from his years in the Army and on the streets, that the world was not safe. He questioned if God really cared about him. He remarked, "I don't think I can trust Him."

Some of you may have discovered that the world wasn't safe early in life, too. Perhaps you had parents who neglected or abused you. Maybe a relative or neighbor took advantage of you. Maybe the foster care system you entered failed you dismally. You may see danger everywhere now and hardships as unavoidable and the norm. Perhaps it is hard for you to trust Him.

Psalm 91 gives us a glimpse of the various sufferings we can expect: *the fowler's snare*, *deadly pestilence*, *the terror of night*, *the arrow that flies by day*, *the pestilence that stalks in the darkness*, *the plague that destroys at midday*, and *a thousand may fall at your side*.

We may experience unrelenting fear, mistreatment, injustice, racism, terrorism, gun violence, or the death of a loved one. We might experience these issues in our homes or at work, on the streets, or in our cars. Morning or night, the pain will come. The psalmist knew this, which is why God doesn't leave us alone, in a pit of despair. Instead, He offers a refuge so secure that we can rest.

There are seasons in our lives, however, when even this comfort doesn't allow us to feel better. Bad things do happen, pain does come, and a personal loss can steal life right out of our hands. We might even wonder where the safety of God is in all this.

The truth is that we all want a life free from pain. We want marriages that don't ever struggle, children who are honor students and obedient, bodies that stay vibrant and healthy, and personal relationships that are friendly, rich, and do not require high maintenance. We do not want conflict; we want safety. However, safety isn't the absence of suffering; safety is finding rest in the middle of it.

An infantry brigade of the U.S. Expeditionary Army in World War I was preparing for combat. Many of the soldiers had never seen the horrors of combat before. Their commander, a devout Christian, called an assembly of his men where he gave each soldier a little card on which was printed the 91st Psalm. They agreed to recite the psalm daily. As word got out, they were nicknamed the "91st Brigade" by other soldiers. The 91st Psalm also became known as, and is still called today, the "Soldier's Psalm." It is important to note the 91st Brigade engaged in three of the war's bloodiest battles. While other American units similarly engaged had up to 90 percent casualties, the 91st Brigade did not suffer a single combat-related casualty.

Choosing God as your safety doesn't mean the struggles will cease. It doesn't silence the thunder or dim the lightning in our lives. In the midst of the darkness in this world, living in it with Jesus and His freedom assures us that we are not walking alone. He never says that we won't face hard times. What He does tell us is that He'll be with us, rescuing us and shining His favor over us. There is no refuge like our God. Right now and forever, our God is willing and able to keep His promises to us.

ENGAGE

Take a few minutes and write out Psalm 91:1-2.

When you are done, read it through as many times as you can, committing it to memory.

End by telling God that He is your refuge, your safety net, and in Him, you put all your trust.

DAY 3

Giants

"As the Philistine moved closer to attack him, David ran quickly toward the battle line to meet him. Reaching into his bag and taking out a stone, he slung it and struck the Philistine on the forehead. The stone sank into his forehead, and he fell facedown on the ground. So David triumphed over the Philistine with a sling and a stone; without a sword in his hand he struck down the Philistine and killed him." 1 Samuel 17:48-50 NIV

In the movie *Hoosiers*, small-town Hickory High School plays in the 1952 Indiana State High School Basketball Championship against a team from a much larger high school in urban South Bend, Indiana. In one scene, the Hickory team walks into the Butler Field House, where the championship game will be played. Butler Field House can hold over 9,000 people.

Coach Norman Dale, played by Gene Hackman, realizes his team is feeling overwhelmed, not only by playing this powerhouse South Bend team but also by the size of the field house. Coach Dale has the players go onto the court and measure the distance from the free throw line to the basket (15 feet) and the height of the basket rim from the floor (10 feet). Coach Dale then remarks, "I assure you that these dimensions are exactly the same as our court in Hickory."

The Hickory team was fighting giants. Giants are projections of our fears. Giants might look like a bad report from your doctor, an ailing parent or spouse, a sudden job loss, a failing marriage, a prodigal child, endless deployments, unemployment, financial issues, and various types of abuse.

Satan loves to create giants in our lives. He loves to whisper in our ears that we cannot defeat them; we are not only helpless but hopelessly overmatched. When speaking of giants, the story of David and Goliath immediately comes to mind.

David showed up to the fight discussing God. He asked the men standing around, "Who does this fool Goliath think he is? How crazy is he to think that he can speak against the armies of the Living God?" David stood up to King Saul and declared that he could destroy Goliath. Regardless of what Saul said, David knew that God would protect him.

He told Saul about how God had delivered him from the paws of the lion and the bear. He declared to everyone that God would deliver him from the hand of this giant too. And He did!

We have a champion in Jesus. Through His death and resurrection, Jesus conquered the giants that seek to destroy us. Jesus is greater than any giant we are facing. Paul writes to the church at Colossi, "Having disarmed the powers and authorities, he made a public spectacle of them, triumphing over them by the cross." (Colossians 2:15)

Life is filled with giants. What is your plan for defeating your giant? Are you going to run, perhaps hide in a corner? Or are you going to pick up your spiritual weapons and fight? The moment we realize that the giants of life may be too big for us is the exact moment we can begin to rest in Christ's rescue.

ENGAGE

Here is a quiz:

Write down all of the giants you
are facing in your life today.

Now cross out the giants that Jesus is
capable of eradicating. Do you see my point?

DAY 4

Ranger Buddy

"Two are better than one . . . one can help the other up . . . But pity anyone who falls and has no one to help them up . . . Though one may be overpowered, two can defend themselves. A cord of three strands is not quickly broken." Ecclesiastes 4:9-12 NIV

I was the Executive Pastor of our church in Boise, Idaho. I had just finishing praying with the worship team and was getting ready to do my final rehearsal for Sunday's message. Gail suddenly came into my office. Her body language spoke sorrow—teary eyes, shoulders dropped, slow pace. My first words were, "Are you okay? Is something wrong with our kids?" I had never seen her so low before.

Gail relayed, "As I was driving into church there was a dead duck lying in the middle of the road. The other cars were negotiating around it. Beside this dead duck was its mate, lying right beside it. It was the saddest thing I ever saw." Gail's words made me tear up.

I went out to remove the dead duck, but some kind soul had already moved the dead duck to a safe grassy area off the road. Its mate was still by its side. The mate may not have completely understood what had happened, but it was not going to leave its best friend alone.

Ranger School is one of the most intense mentally and physically challenging schools in the Army. It is an eight-week regimen of constant movement, parachute jumps, rubber raft trips in swamps and salt water, climbing mountains, daily eight- to ten-mile hikes carrying everything on your back, eating one meager meal a day, and maybe sleeping less than two hours each day—maybe.

When I went to this school, I was assigned a "ranger buddy" on day one. Bill Harlan and I were to navigate this hellish course together. We became like brothers. We decided we would cross the finish line eight weeks later together or we would not cross it at all. Eight weeks later, Bill and I shook hands as we finished Ranger School together. Just like ducks and Army Rangers, as God's sons and daughters, we too are created for community.

King Solomon describes and warns us how vulnerable we are when we try to go through life alone. Solomon writes that God never intended for you and me to be alone, vulnerable, or isolated. We need relationships with each other for encouragement, refreshment, renewal, and growth. I think in retrospect this is why the pandemic, with the social distancing and concomitant isolation, was and still remains so difficult for many of us.

We have to learn, innovate, experiment, and try different ways to reach out, to share burdens, to console grieving hearts, and to demonstrate love.

ENGAGE

Who do you know who could use a word of encouragement today? Pray to God and ask Him to help you to see someone in your sphere of influence who might need you to be their ranger buddy. How can you encourage, refresh, renew, and help a friend grow? You both will be stronger for it.

DAY 5

The Power to Choose

"And if it is evil in your eyes to serve the Lord, choose this day whom you will serve, whether the gods your fathers served in the region beyond the River, or the gods of the Amorites in whose land you dwell. But as for me and my house, we will serve the Lord." Joshua 24:15 ESV

As soldiers, we live out our choices every day. What we say, what we believe, where we work, who we support, and what we ignore are all choices we get to make. With each choice comes responsibility and accountability, but some of us disregard these in the name of having the choice.

We make choices every day that have minor consequences of substance, such as the shampoo we use, what we wear, and at what stores we shop. We also experience choices that may have significant ramifications on our lives and the lives of others, such as choosing to pay our taxes, choosing to abort a baby, choosing to use drugs or alcohol as an escape from reality, choosing to disobey a lawful order, or choosing to break the law.

Last week I met with a young veteran who had a choice to make. He told me he needed to decide if he should disclose some very private and personal information from his past in order to be considered for a job. He told me no one, except for him, knew of this information. He knew the information might prevent him from even getting past the interview. However, if he was later found out to have not disclosed this info, he could be in serious trouble. He had gone to several people who told him to hide the info and not disclose it for fear of losing this opportunity. He then solicited my counsel.

I shared with him a verse from the Book of Proverbs that says, "Whoever walks in integrity walks securely, but whoever takes crooked paths will be found out." (Proverbs 10:9 NIV) I encouraged him not to hide the info. I suggested he choose to tell the truth and let God determine what path his potential employer would take.

Many in our society do not choose to accept responsibility for their actions. We see this every day and the concomitant impact these choices have on their children, families, and institutions. Some blame society. Others blame the environment. Many blame the schools or political parties. Some even blame God. We can't blame it all on somebody else, but oh, how we try!

We must accept responsibility for our choices and decisions. Taking responsibility for your choices requires the realization that each of us plays an integral part in every situation or experience and, therefore, we all have some degree of responsibility over the outcomes or consequences.

You made the decision to serve your nation, to fight its wars, and to ensure liberty and freedom for all people, even if your decision ends up costing you your life. Many in our nation do not share your courage and commitment to take this honorable and selfless step. Thank you.

ENGAGE

What choices are you faced with right now? Is there an easy choice? Which one is right? Have you considered asking Jesus to be the leader of your life? God has given us the power of choice. When you are not absolutely certain which choice to make, ask God to help you discern the right path.

DAY 6

Signal Mirrors

"For you were once darkness, but now you are light in the Lord. Live as children of light." Ephesians 5:8 NIV

During my Army career, we often used light to help our units maneuver and defeat our enemies. Illumination artillery and mortar rounds would help us see the enemy positions or potential obstacles in our path during night operations. We would use light to read our maps for navigation, and signal flares in the sky might tell us to start the attack, cease firing our weapons, or begin to withdraw. As technology advanced, night vision devices captured available light on a digital image sensor and then digitally enhanced the images in a display that helped us see in the dark.

During certain daylight operations, when we did not want to use our radios or other electronic devices that might give away our positions to the enemy, we might use sunlight and mirrors to communicate. For example, using the power of the sun, we might position our hand-held mirror to create a flash of light to tell other units we were at a specific location or to signal approaching aircraft to land at a certain location.

Light is mentioned hundreds of times and in dozens of ways throughout both the Old and the New Testaments, but trying to define light is similar to defining love. To me the simplest way to describe light is to say that light illuminates or makes visible what is already there.

Jesus said that He is the light of the world; He is God made known, unveiled, revealed, and visible. When God opens the eyes of our hearts and minds and makes Jesus visible to us, we begin relating to and interacting with our heavenly Father through Jesus in the way that He personally designed us to do. The Apostle Paul tells us that because we now interact with and know God, He also calls and empowers us to interact with everybody else in His creation in the way He designed us.

If you really look at your community, many people are living in despair and darkness; they do not know Jesus and are living without His hope. I believe God calls us to be a part of these people's lives. He calls us to be light, to model and live out what a light-filled life is like. In turn, He invites those who are still in darkness to step out of it and into His amazing light.

If you question whether you have the right skill sets to do so, please remember these two facts: our signal mirrors had no power of their own, and they used the power of the Sun to shine light. We have the power to shine light in a dark world because we are empowered by the Son.

This week, why not do what a favorite children's song tells us? "This little light of mine, I'm gonna make it shine, make it shine, make it shine, make it shine." Let's live as children of light.

ENGAGE

Are you ready to commit to reach out to those friends, relatives, neighbors, and coworkers living in despair and darkness, absent of hope? How can you shine God's light on them this week? Write down three ways you can bring hope to people who are struggling in the darkness this week.

DAY 7

Death Zone

"But David remained at Jerusalem." 2 Samuel 11:1 ESV

In Ranger School, we climbed and rappelled the Blue Ridge mountains located near Camp Merrill, Dahlonega, Georgia. I have always been intrigued by climbing mountains. Gail and I have hiked "14ers" in Colorado, our son and I climbed Mount Rainier in Washington, and our youngest daughter and I climbed Mount Borah in Idaho. I even had delusions that one day I would climb the Himalayas.

As I grew older (and saner), I knew my skill set would never be such that I could climb Mount Everest. As you might know, climbers who ascend higher than 26,000 feet on Mount Everest enter what is called the Death Zone. In this zone, oxygen is so limited that the cells in your body start to die; one's judgment becomes severely impaired. In the Death Zone, climbers can experience acute altitude sickness, lethal brain swelling, heart attacks, strokes, and death.

I recently read that twelve people have already died, and five are missing on Everest just as the 2023 spring climbing season comes to an end. It is very dangerous at the top! The Death Zone is real.

We can see very similar death zones when people are seeking success, notoriety, and celebrity. Fame and celebrity can closely mirror substance abuse and, over time, may result in actual substance abuse, isolation, mistrust, dysfunctional adaptation to fame, and too often, untimely death. The examples are familiar: Whitney Houston, River Phoenix, Heath Ledger, and Michael Jackson.

We can also see it in fallen ministry leaders who stay in the "Death Zone" too long, such as pastors Bill Hybels, Jim Bakker, Ted Haggard, and Hillsong's Brian Houston. The Death Zone is not discriminatory; it can affect business leaders, politicians, Hollywood stars, military leaders, and people from all walks of life, incomes, ethnic origins, races, and faiths.

Recent research shows that fame and celebrity can change a person's life forever. Some descriptions of fame include feeling like an animal in a cage, a toy in a shop window, a Barbie doll, a public façade, and a clay figure. Many fame seekers believe everything that is written about them is true and never see the stark reality of being in the Death Zone.

In the Bible, David survived his dangerous and arduous climb to the top. He killed lions and bears, fought and killed Goliath, avoided Saul's pursuing army, and conquered other nations to become king. The prophet Samuel wrote that the Lord gave David victory wherever he went. However, David lingered on the mountaintop and stayed in the Death Zone too long.

When his army set out on a new mission, he made the conscious decision to remain in Jerusalem. He relished the accolades of his triumphs and enjoyed basking in the public limelight. It was during this same time that he committed adultery with Bathsheba and contrived the wicked plan to have her husband, Uriah, murdered.

It's hard to stay grounded when your friends, peers, and even your commanders fawn over you and tell you that you're incredibly gifted, talented, and special. If you've achieved some modicum of success, perhaps in the military or in life after your service, you may appropriately celebrate the accomplishment and, in turn, humbly thank God for His gifts and blessings, but you must not forget to keep moving down the mountain. We must realize when we are in the Death Zone. We need to come down and humbly serve others in the valley, so to speak, asking God to guard our hearts and our next steps. Staying in the Death Zone can be hazardous to our lives.

ENGAGE

Are you in the Death Zone? Do you believe your own press clippings? Are you enthralled by what other people say about how extraordinary and special you are?

If so, first give all the glory to God, then move off the summit, venture into the valleys, and begin serving others with these same gifts and talents. Ask God to help you see how lingering in the Death Zone too long can set you up for disaster. Write down your prayer.

DAY 8

A Cup of Decaf

"Put on then, as God's chosen ones, holy and beloved, compassionate hearts, kindness, humility, meekness, and patience." Colossians 3:12 ESV

Driving home a few weeks ago, I listened to a radio program titled "Unsung Heroes." The program captures ordinary citizens sharing how one person or organization was kind, generous, loving, and patient with them. I listened to a story about how a car dealership helped a single mom with a malfunctioning car. The team at the dealership took the mom to work and her eight-year-old daughter to school while they fixed the car. When the car was repaired, the dealership staff picked up the mom and did not charge her for any parts or labor.

In my time in uniform, I saw numerous unsung heroes protect innocent civilians who were in harm's way. Time and time again, I saw soldiers give their water and food to starving children in the area of operation. After an intense firefight, I saw medics caring for the injured enemy soldiers, in the same manner they would have cared for their peers. I was humbled by their sense of duty, compassion, and caring.

We experienced another unsung hero during a recent trip when Gail and I flew home from a week-long vacation in Colorado. We got to the airport early in the morning, checked in, and decided to have breakfast before we boarded. We ordered our food, and our first waitress asked us what we would like to drink. I asked for black coffee, and Gail asked if they had decaf. This waitress said, "No, we do not have decaf." Gail replied, "Okay, I'll just have water then. Thank you."

Another waitress, named Desiree, who was waiting on another table, overheard our first waitress and told Gail, "I will make a pot for you." About five minutes later, Desiree brought out a hot cup of decaf for Gail. We both thanked Desiree for her kindness.

We experienced an unsung hero that day. The Apostle Paul wrote to the church at Colossi that, as chosen ones, they were to act kindly and be compassionate to others. I believe these words were also clearly written for you and me to follow today.

The Word of God continuously reminds us to be kind by being compassionate to one another. If someone requires help, whether emotionally or physically, we are told in His Word to be kind and lend a helping hand.

We are to be kind because Jesus is kind to us. It really does not matter how small or big our kindness may be; all kindness has the same face. What truly matters is that we show kindness and compassion in whatever possible and tangible ways we can each day.

Desiree obviously gets it. How about you? Are you an unsung hero? Do you show love to, care for, and/or assist others, even folks you do not know and may never fully know? Your efforts and kindness may not be fully appreciated now, but please know your reward will be in Heaven.

ENGAGE

Who in your life needs help or needs you to come alongside them? Write down a list of ways you can be an unsung hero to your neighbor, fellow soldier, family member, or complete stranger. As you go through the day, keep your eyes open for opportunities.

DAY 9

Adversity

"Though the Lord gave you adversity for food and suffering for drink, He will still be with you to teach you." Isaiah 30:20 NLT

I was speaking to a wonderful Army friend last week. He shared he had more than his fair share of adversity this past year. He lost his job, contracted COVID-19, and stated his son was "going south" in his behavior and associating with the wrong crowd.

No person is exempt from adversity. Trouble shows up daily and comes in different shapes, intensities, and sizes, including hardship, misery, and outright failure. Adversity can range from a small setback to a full-blown, life-threatening disaster.

Our usual response to adversity is either to complain about the situation, blame others for the difficulty, or get angry at our ineptness to exercise control. Some of us might act as if nothing has happened, others may completely deny that the adversity exists, while others become discouraged and give up.

When we face adversity or are in the midst of its grip, we oftentimes fail to understand that adversity can teach us some insightful lessons for navigating life.

The prophet Isaiah tells us that God uses adversity to teach us how to live His way. Every step we take through a trial or difficulty according to His purpose will help us to grow in Him. We learn to depend on Him for everything and begin to understand that adverse situations can be real blessings in disguise that increase our faith and help us develop courage, faith, and trust in God.

Even though adverse conditions are painful, we can remain confident and optimistic that God is always in control. We learn that what matters is not the adverse events or the difficult people we must endure during troubled times, but rather what we can learn from God. As we endure and suffer through adversity, the lessons God teaches us will have life-changing and eternal impact. As my friend shared at the end of our conversation, "Through it all, I knew God was in control. I now have a better job, I am now healthy, and my son is making better choices." Citing from John's 16th chapter, my friend concluded, "You know, Tom, Jesus was right, 'In this world you will have trouble. But take heart! I have overcome the world.'" (v33)

As soldiers and military families, we can face adversity every day. Demanding, rigorous training and frequent separations from loved ones are challenging even during times of peace. The specter of actual combat presents added stressors. The palpable fear of death or significant, debilitating injury to ourselves or fellow soldiers, the moral and ethical challenges inherent in war, and prolonged absences from friends and family contribute to the stressors of our profession and lifestyle. All of that can challenge the mental health and stability of soldiers and their families.

I challenge you to listen with your ears, watch with your eyes, and feel with your heart what God is doing in and through you during these times of adversity. It is important to remember that He has overcome the world!

ENGAGE

If you are facing adversity today, what lessons are you learning about God's faithfulness and His love for you? Write down the adversity and next to it, what God can teach you through it. Pray that each hardship will lead to your personal growth and faith.

DAY 10

Anchored

"I will fasten him like a peg in a secure place, and he will become a throne of honor to his father's house." Isaiah 22:23 ESV

Gail and I have had the great fortune to live in two historic homes: one at the U.S. Military Academy at West Point, New York, and another in Ontario, Oregon. Both homes were close to 100 years old. Our homes had great character, including hardwood floors, high ceilings, large windows, wonderfully textured plaster walls, and actual cloth affixed to the walls.

We were cautioned that to hang the many pictures we own or Gail has painted, we would have to either drill the nail into a wood support or use a special plaster anchor nail for support. Otherwise, our art might crash to the floor, leaving an unsightly hole behind.

The prophet Isaiah used the imagery of a nail driven firmly into a wall to describe a Biblical character named Eliakim. Unlike his predecessor, the corrupt and notorious leader Shebna, Eliakim trusted in God. Isaiah prophesied that Eliakim would become prime minister in Judah for King Hezekiah. Isaiah wrote that Eliakim, whose name meant "God will establish" or "God rises," would be driven "like a peg into a secure place." Securely anchored in God's truth and grace, Isaiah knew Eliakim would provide the fair and just leadership that his family and his people needed.

You and I live in a world that suffers because of sin. However, one fact is certain: God is still in control. Time and time again in Scripture, God reminds us that all things work together for good if we love God.

Sin separates us from God. No spiritually good thing dwells in us or can proceed from us. We all must humble ourselves to the mercies of God and recognize a need to be anchored in the Lord.

Friends in the Navy have told me the purpose of an anchor is to keep a ship safe and secure at a desired location or to help control the ship during inclement weather. However, to accomplish these vital purposes, just having an anchor is not enough. The anchor must be solid, dependable, and used properly at the right time and place. Isaiah concluded this prophecy with a sobering reminder that no person can be the ultimate security for friends or family. We all fail and fall short. The only completely trustworthy anchor for our lives is Jesus. He is the sure and steadfast anchor of our souls.

Perhaps in the past weeks, you have let a teammate down, disappointed your spouse, or unknowingly let your child down. Maybe you thought you were anchored in your own strength, your own confidence, arrogance, or pride. As much as we try not to, we will let people down. Each of us is human with frailties and shortcomings. However, when you and I care for others and share their burdens, we point them to God, the anchor who will never fail.

ENGAGE

Today, anchor yourself to God. Pray today,
asking and allowing Him to be your strength,
your firm foundation; your anchor.

DAY 11

Civic Virtue

"So if there is any encouragement in Christ, any comfort from love, any participation in the Spirit, any affection and sympathy, complete my joy by being of the same mind, having the same love, being in full accord and of one mind. Do nothing from selfish ambition or conceit, but in humility count others more significant than yourselves. Let each of you look not only to his own interests, but also to the interests of others." Philippians 2:1-4 ESV

One of the key concepts our nation's founding fathers used to base their decisions on was "civic virtue," or the personal devotion to the success of the community. These patriots argued that a successful society required citizens who lived more for each other than for personal interests.

Realizing that being a colony of the British Empire prevented this, our leaders created the moral and logical justification for the American Revolution. They went to war knowing they were all in it together. As Benjamin Franklin said, "We must, indeed, all hang together or, most assuredly, we shall all hang separately."

As soldiers, we live this ethos every day. Teamwork and selflessness are paramount to our unit's mission success. We rely on each other on and off the battlefield. Indeed, working together as a team can forge a force far superior to our individual capabilities.

Much has changed since our nation's founding. Today we see political power plays happening almost every day. We see politicians from both parties refusing to compromise on various and much-needed legislation, seeking to change the rules just to get their way, and living out a reckless and insane drive to pursue power and prestige regardless of the overall and perhaps permanent damage to the republic.

Political power plays are, unfortunately, a tragic part of history. King David's third son, Absalom, followed his pride and greed and tried to seize his father's throne. He was killed by David's soldiers for his act of treason. King David's fourth son, Adonijah, recruited David's leading general and priest to make himself king. David, however, had chosen Solomon as king. A rebellion ensued. David, with the help of the prophet Nathan, subdued the rebellion, and David even forgave Adonijah for his act. However, pride, arrogance, and greed pushed Adonijah to plot a second insurrection to steal the throne from his brother and now king, Solomon. Solomon had Adonijah executed.

God created us with unique talents and gifts. To ignore this fact and say we should all act and be the same would be unwise and would demean God's own creativity. On the other hand, if we put our individuality above God's plan for us to be a part of His church, then we make an idol of our uniqueness. I have often heard it said that if "being you" hurts others and draws attention away from Christ, then maybe you're being the wrong you.

The Apostle Paul tells the church at Philippi that selfishly pursuing their own ambitions never brings to them their truest, deepest longings. Leaving the outcome to God is the only path to peace and joy.

ENGAGE

Today, please pray about, reflect, and write out your honest responses to these three questions that get to the heart of Paul's desire for complete joy:

Do you care more about how people see you or about how people see Christ in your life?

Do people feel encouraged after spending time with you?

How well do you serve the needs of the people around you?

DAY 12

A Gentle Answer

"A soft answer turns away wrath, but a harsh word stirs up anger. The tongue of the wise commends knowledge, but the mouths of fools pour out folly. The eyes of the Lord are in every place, keeping watch on the evil and the good. A gentle tongue is a tree of life, but perverseness in it breaks the spirit." Proverbs 15:1-4 ESV

On a recent vacation to France, Gail and I decided to take the Paris Metro to get from one part of the city to another. Like most metropolitan systems, our train car was extremely crowded. As the door closed at one of our stops, we could hear two men talking very loudly to each other. Since they were speaking French, we had no idea what they were discussing, but all of us on the train car could tell the discussion was getting very heated.

A young woman next to me looked both irritated and embarrassed that her fellow Parisians were speaking so loudly and rudely at each other. Gail and I left the train car at the next stop; we both hoped sanity and civil, nonviolent behavior would prevail between these two gentlemen.

We have all seen people who will sometimes use harsh words with accelerating and increasing vocal volume during a conflict. These people often exhibit anger and resort to shouting to confirm their respective point or opinion. As an outsider, their behavior can be viewed as childish, immature, or simply arrogant.

In the Book of Proverbs, King Solomon shares some wise advice for times like these: "A gentle answer turns away wrath, but a harsh word stirs up anger." He goes on to say, "A gentle tongue is a tree of life."

Disagreements, arguments, and conflict can often be a part of our everyday lives. Whether it is our views on decisions our governmental leaders have made, how and what we should educate our children on, or sometimes mundane issues such as what we should have for dinner, these differences can draw us into a conflict or disagreement.

In looking at how Jesus lived, He provided you and me two reasons for gently appealing to those with whom we might otherwise enter into conflict or disagreement. First, we need to extend love that reveals us to be His children, and second, seek reconciliation in order to win them over.

In early December, I watched the Army-Navy football game. It was its usual back-and-forth, hard-fought game until it went into overtime for the first time in the game's 123-year history. In fact, it went into double overtime, with Army eventually scoring the field goal that won the game. What really impressed me was when the two head coaches, Navy's Ken Niumatalolo and Army's Jeff Monken, met at mid-field after the game and hugged each other.

There was no animosity, bitterness, hatred, or harsh words shared. It was simply two coaches demonstrating love and respect to each other while honoring that their respective teams played their hearts out that day. On the field in Philadelphia on that Saturday, the world saw in both men how Jesus would act.

ENGAGE

Do you feel you have to always win an argument? Remember that honest people do not need to be disagreeable. When getting heated about a conflict, consider allowing God to guide you by and through the Holy Spirit to show love, civility, and wisdom to others. Write down your prayer, asking God to help you show love to others—especially if you have a disagreement.

DAY 13

Consistency is Key

> "And let us not grow weary of doing good, for in due season we will reap, if we do not give up." Galatians 6:9 ESV

I recently met with the CEO of a very successful and highly respected rescue mission. As we discussed the various ministries and services the mission offers to addicts, homeless veterans, men, women, and lost souls in search of their life's purpose, he looked me in the eye and told me, "Consistency is absolutely crucial to everything we do. If we say dinner is at 6 p.m., then we must ensure dinner is at 6 p.m. If we say you can take a shower at 8 a.m., then we must ensure the shower is available at 8 a.m. Consistency builds trust, and trust opens the door to meaningful and life-changing conversations."

In your unit or workplace, your peers and/or soldiers expect consistency. Otherwise, they can become exasperated and frustrated by your constantly changing character or mood. Likewise, as parents, our children need our behavior to be consistent so they can feel safe and secure.

Having consistency brings stability. Consistency in your behavior reflects and demonstrates to others your personal integrity.

Be constantly in the presence of Christ in prayer and read His Word. This will help you realize that you are totally and wholly His. The Word tells us that living for Jesus requires holiness; He will bless your consistent "right living."

Being consistent in doing what is right will grow your integrity. Consistent character and behavior will afford you credibility, respect, and ultimately influence. Following through with your word may be exactly what wins a friend over to Christ.

Doing what is right in every situation can be costly in terms of friendships, relationships, and finances, but inconsistency will always weaken your credibility and reputation. Conforming to Christ's character, not to the world's ever-changing and unstable way of living, is not always easy.

General Norman Schwarzkopf, CINC of all U.S. and allied forces in Operation Desert Storm, spoke to our leadership team a day before we launched our attack into Iraq. General Schwarzkopf spoke to us about consistency. He stated, "Integrity is who you are when only God is watching."

Do you do what is right even when no one can see you? Is your word your bond? Are your decisions and concomitant actions consistent with what you said you would do? With God as our helper, when we constantly do what is right, when our every action and spoken word are congruent and consistent, I believe people will see Jesus in you and me. Our consistent behavior will bring blessings to them and to us.

ENGAGE

Think about people in your life that have been an example of integrity and steadfastness to you. Pray and ask God to help you be consistent in your actions and speech.

DAY 14

Worth

"O Lord, you have searched me and known me! You know when I sit down and when I rise up; you discern my thoughts from afar. You search out my path and my lying down and are acquainted with all my ways. Even before a word is on my tongue, behold, O Lord, you know it altogether. You hem me in, behind and before, and lay your hand upon me. Such knowledge is too wonderful for me; it is high; I cannot attain it." Psalm 139:1-6 ESV

During the aftermath of 9/11, the September 11th Victim Compensation Fund was created by an Act of Congress in 2001 to compensate the victims of the attack or their families in exchange for their agreement not to sue the airline corporations involved. Kenneth Feinberg was appointed by the President to be special master of the fund. He developed the regulations governing the administration of the fund and administered all aspects of the program. The legislation authorized the fund to disburse a maximum of $7.375

billion, including operational and administrative costs, of U.S. government funds. Feinberg's challenge was how to determine a person's worth.

Initially, Feinberg tried to use standard actuary tables and life income projections in trying to face the impossible task of determining the worth of a life to help the families who had suffered incalculable losses. Many of the affected families felt Mr. Feinberg lacked empathy. When Mr. Feinberg locked horns with Mr. Charles Wolf, a community organizer mourning the death of his wife, his initial cynicism turned to compassion as he began to learn the true human costs of the tragedy. This demonstrated a heartfelt compassion that touched many families. These families then felt valued and allowed Mr. Feinberg to resolve and pay 97% of the affected families for their loss.

Along similar lines, the book and later the movie titled *Moneyball* chronicled the life of the Oakland Athletics baseball team and its General Manager, Billy Beane. Mr. Beane literally invented the use of statistics and data-driven decisions to scout talent, choose players, and turn a losing team around. The conventional wisdom of a consortium of coaches, general managers, and sports journalists at that time had rigid conceptions of what makes a good player and how teams win games. Mr. Beane turned this wisdom on its ear.

Due to his limited budget, Mr. Beane turned to overlooked and undervalued players. These were players discarded due to factors such as age and personality. Using Mr. Beane's methodology, the team won 20 games in a row, setting a major league record. The team also won the American League West in 2002 with a record of 103-59. He assembled a gaggle of talented and gifted misfits who offered crucial skills at various times to win baseball games. He made these "misfits" feel valued.

Our core emotional need is to feel valued. How we perceive our value and worth are incredibly important. Self-worth is defined by *Merriam-Webster* dictionary as "the sense of one's value or worth as a person." Self-worth, or the lack of it, is at the root of all positive and negative behavior. There is nothing more critical than self-worth in determining our success or failure. How much are you worth?

Typically, in response to the question of worth, we think of money, don't we? We look at our bank accounts, stock portfolios, the size of our houses, what we drive or even age and physical appearance. The problem with determining our value this way is that we always come up short. Someone will always have more money and a bigger house, our looks will fade, and our waistlines will expand. I suggest that we base our value on a different perspective.

The psalmist underscores and presents the most reasonable and compelling argument for our worth and the value God places on us. God knows us as we are.

DAY 14

Nothing about your life is hidden from God. God is involved in the circumstances and affairs of your life.

When we are known, we experience value.

Have you ever walked into a crowded event where no one knows you? How did it make you feel? On the other hand, have you ever walked into a party where you are known, or better yet, the party was for you?

With God, you are the center of His attention. God has always been thinking of you, before birth, during birth, through childhood, into adolescence, and on through adulthood. He never stops thinking of you. You are of incredible value and worth to Him. Jesus's death on the cross and resurrection for your sins and mine are evidence of this incredible love.

ENGAGE

Right now, thank God for knowing and loving you. Talk to Him and thank Him for your family, your position, your profession, and your life.

DAY 15

My Banner is Clear

"Only let your manner of life be worthy of the gospel of Christ, so that whether I come and see you or am absent, I may hear of you that you are standing firm in one spirit, with one mind striving side by side for the faith of the gospel." Philippians 1:27 ESV

As I was preparing to speak one Sunday on living out your faith, I was brainstorming with a friend about how to challenge our church members listening to my message. Using my military experiences and background, I shared this crazy idea to have a friend dress up in a ninja outfit carrying an unloaded military-style weapon. As we began singing and worshipping, I thought the "ninja" would enter the worship center in a loud manner, tell everyone to sit down, and then ask in a mean and menacing voice, "Who is a Christian in this room?" My idea was to see if anyone would be willing to say so, in spite of the possibility that the "ninja" might just shoot the person who stood up.

As I shared this idea with a friend, he looked at me like I was crazy. He said, "Do you know how many of our members have Idaho concealed carry licenses? If you tried this, the church would look like the *Gunfight at the OK Corral* movie. It would be pure carnage." We both laughed, and I replied, "So much for my creativity."

This insane skit, however, does present an interesting question. How does anyone know you are a follower of Jesus? Is it because you wear a cross necklace? Or is it because you have a fish sticker on your car's bumper? Or maybe you keep a Bible on your desk at work? The only real way for us, as humans, to know if someone is truly a Christian is to observe a person's life on the outside. Since we cannot see the interior of their heart as God does, our only choice is to look for some exterior result or indicator of their faith.

In our home, I have an Avery T. Willis, Jr. quote framed and sitting on my desk. I read it almost every day as a personal challenge to stand firm in my faith. Allow me to share what Mr. Willis wrote:

> I'm part of the fellowship of the unashamed. I have Holy Spirit power. The die has been cast. I have stepped over the line. The decision has been made. I'm a disciple of His. I won't look back, let up, slow down, back away, or be still. My past is redeemed, my present makes sense, my future is secure. I'm finished and done with low living, sight walking, small planning, smooth knees, colorless

dreams, tamed visions, mundane talking, cheap living, and dwarfed goals. I no longer need prominence, prosperity, position, promotions, plaudits, or popularity. I don't have to be right, first, tops, recognized, praised, regarded, or rewarded. I now live by faith, lean on His presence, walk by patience, lift by prayer, and labor by power. My face is set, my gait is fast, my goal is heaven, my road is narrow, my way is rough, my companions are few, my Guide is reliable, my mission is clear. I cannot be bought, compromised, detoured, lured away, turned back, deluded, or delayed. I will not flinch in the face of sacrifice, hesitate in the presence of the adversary, negotiate at the table of the enemy, ponder at the pool of popularity, or meander in the maze of mediocrity. I won't give up, shut up, let up, until I have stayed up, stored up, prayed up, paid up, and preached up for the cause of Christ. I am a disciple of Jesus. I must go till He comes, give till I drop, preach till all know, and work till He stops me. And when He comes for His own, He will have no problem recognizing me—my banner will be clear.

ENGAGE

Look at your uniforms today. Look at the patches on your arms and chest. Look at the ribbons and medals you might be wearing. What do these patches and ribbons say or not say about you?

Now consider if Jesus would recognize you as His disciple. Is your past redeemed? Does your present makes sense? Is your future secure? If you are not sure, talk to God today, giving him your whole life and future.

DAY 16

Less Bark, More Wag

> "One of the teachers of the law came and heard them debating. Noticing that Jesus had given them a good answer, he asked him, 'Of all the commandments, which is the most important?'
>
> 'The most important one,' answered Jesus, 'is this: 'Hear, O Israel: The Lord our God, the Lord is one. Love the Lord your God with all your heart and with all your soul and with all your mind and with all your strength.' The second is this: 'Love your neighbor as yourself.' There is no commandment greater than these.'" Mark 12:28-31 NIV

On a recent visit to our local dog food store, I saw a sign saying, "Less Bark, More Wag." It reminded me of our dog, Holly. Our chocolate lab loves what I call Dog World, a fenced park in our hometown that allows dogs to be off-leash, running and playing together. Holly sprints out of the car when we get to this park and upon her entry, immediately begins to socialize with all the dogs who are present. The breed, size, or color of the other dogs isn't even in Holly's decision process. With her tail wagging, she meets many dogs who respond to her in a similar manner. Once in a while, she will encounter a dog that growls at her and wants her to stay away. Holly realizes this dog might have a problem and moves away to befriend a more friendly dog.

I suspect we have people in our lives whom we enjoy seeing and being with for extended periods of time. I suspect there might also be other people we try to avoid or not engage with for various reasons.

Jesus explained the two greatest commandments are to love God and to love your neighbor as yourself. A neighbor is not just the person next door, but everyone around you. This revelation would be upsetting to the Pharisees and Sadducees, especially because they made their fortune through people giving them offerings and sacrifices for their mistakes.

What Jesus was sharing here is that if we love God with everything we have and share that love with those around us, it is the greatest offering God could ask for. When we place God above all else and share His love with those around us, it pleases Him.

It is also important to remember that to love your neighbor as yourself implies you need to be cognizant of the love God has for you first. Jesus died for you in order for you to be freed from sin and become the person God intended you to be. If you don't realize all the sacrifices God made for you, loving others in the same way He has loved you can be difficult.

As a young Infantry Lieutenant, I remember seeing a young infantry squad leader barking out orders loudly and with a slew of profanities, treating his soldiers like they were not intelligent human beings, and intimidating them into doing the task at hand. My Platoon Sergeant, Sergeant First Class (SFC) Curtis Ray, was standing by my side. He immediately excused himself and went over to coach this squad leader. In a calm and almost fatherly manner, SFC Ray counseled the young leader. Both men shook hands after a few minutes. SFC Ray later told me that his counsel to this young, developing squad leader was "to not raise his voice, but rather raise his expectations." SFC Ray showed love that day to this young leader. I never forgot this incredible lesson.

Loving difficult people is hard. However, when you and I can release everyone and everything to God, our hearts then have the space to offer grace to the next person. Remember, it's not about you or me; it's about others and who they are. Accepting them as Jesus does creates the space to love them well. When you and I do that, the Kingdom advances another step forward. Let that one thought sink in. When we love others as we love ourselves, the Kingdom of God advances!

ENGAGE

Give your time, talent, or treasure this week to someone who doesn't deserve it. They will be blessed and so will you. Try to mimic Holly: less bark, more wag!

DAY 17

Never Quit

"See, I have delivered Jericho into your hands." Joshua 6:2 NIV

Have you ever quit too soon? I was teaching an online college class several years ago. A student in her third year of college called and told me she was ready to trash her dream of getting her college degree. She was a combat veteran and physically suffered from a battle wound that had not properly healed. She was the only caregiver for her two elderly, invalid parents and was working a menial job for minimum wage while going to college.

I tried several times to tell her to hang in there and assure her that God had a plan for her. She blew me off. Later that week, she called again. She was really feeling sorry for herself and started whining to me. I tried to talk to her again, but with every word of encouragement, she responded with a counter-complaint.

Frustrated and tired of hearing her excuses, I lost it and spoke to her like a soldier, saying, "Suck it up and get moving. You are better than this!" I admit that my counseling skills need a ton of work. She hung up on me. I tried repeatedly to call and text message her; I did not hear from her for over a year.

The next year at the college graduation ceremony, she walked up to me, hugged me, and whispered that she realized she needed to hear me say those words to her. We both laughed and shed tears at the same time. I was so proud of her.

We all have times when we want to quit when what we really need is to press on. Sometimes we grow tired of the struggle and tired of trying. I suspect many of us may have missed incredible blessings because we surrendered and said, "I don't want to do this any longer."

The battle plan for Joshua to take the city of Jericho was as simple as it was strange: marching for seven days around the city with an entire army shouting and priests blowing trumpets. To the average person, it was a crazy plan. God's infinite ways often don't make sense to us. Jericho was a fortress and a formidable challenge. Sometimes it can feel like our dreams are as well. That doesn't mean we give up. Rather it means we suit up, step up, and keep moving forward.

God didn't tell Joshua, "I will deliver Jericho into your hands." He said, "I have delivered Jericho into your hands." He had already done it, but the Israelites had to obey His battle plan to win—to receive the blessing of victory.

The Israelites walked around Jericho for six days, and as far as they could tell, nothing happened. This is where many might give up, but God said, "Keep walking by faith."

What do you do when all you see is a Grand Canyon-sized chasm between your dream and your present situation? Just because you don't see God working does not mean He isn't. Paul wrote to the new church at Galatia, "Let us not become weary in doing good, for at the proper time we will reap a harvest if we do not give up." (Galatians 6:9 NIV)

Today, you might be on trek number seven around your "Jericho" and not even know it. Suppose Israel had stopped on day six, saying, "This is stupid, Joshua. We are going back to Egypt. We are not walking another day." They would have missed an incredible blessing.

ENGAGE

How many times might we have missed the blessing because we stopped too soon? Don't give up. If you are in a Jericho situation today, ask God to fill you with the power of the Holy Spirit on the inside, so you can reap a harvest on the outside.

DAY 18

Always There

"And going a little farther he fell on his face and prayed, saying, 'My Father, if it be possible, let this cup pass from me; nevertheless, not as I will, but as you will.'" Matthew 26:39 ESV

Last week we spoke to Jessie, our oldest daughter, about her daughter Celia's trip to the doctor and how Celia hates inoculations. We had to laugh because when Jessie was very young, she also did not really like going to the doctor's office, especially if the visit would end with a "surprise announcement" by the doctor that she needed an inoculation.

Jessie would look at Gail and me and exclaim, "Why wasn't I told about the shot? I cannot get it. I am not prepared!" She would plead with us in great drama and tears, "Mom and Dad, isn't there another way? Can't we just wait until our next visit? Please, Dad, Mom, I don't want to have this shot."

It just about broke our hearts, but we told her, "Jessie, I'm sorry, there's no other way." We would hold her as the doctor or nurse would prepare the shot. Jessie would twist and squirm, wanting to see how big the needle was, as if knowing the needle size was going to really calm her fears.

We couldn't take her pain away; the best we could offer was to be present with her. Tears would often well up in our eyes as she would scream and cry as the needle went into her.

As I was thinking about this minor family crisis, it brought to mind Jesus in the garden of Gethsemane, asking His Father for a different way. How it must have broken the Father's heart to see His beloved Son, in His humanness, and in such agony! Yet God knew there was no other way to save His people.

We sometimes face unavoidable yet painful moments, just like our daughter did. But because of Jesus's work for us through His Spirit, even in our darkest moments, our loving heavenly Father is always present with us.

Charles Spurgeon, a 19th-century English pastor, once said, "God is too good to be unkind, too wise to be mistaken; and when you cannot trace His hand, you can trust His heart."

I am blessed to have a wonderful Idaho friend who wrote to me yesterday and offered, "Do not worry about tomorrow, Jesus is already there."

ENGAGE

Do you believe my friend's words? Thank God today. Write a prayer and then say it aloud to our Father in Heaven. Thank Him for always being there for you.

DAY 19

A Road Not Taken

"Blessed is the man who walks not in the counsel of the wicked, nor stands in the way of sinners, nor sits in the seat of scoffers; but his delight is in the law of the Lord, and on his law he meditates day and night. He is like a tree planted by streams of water that yields its fruit in its season, and its leaf does not wither. In all that he does, he prospers. The wicked are not so but are like chaff that the wind drives away. Therefore the wicked will not stand in the judgment, nor sinners in the congregation of the righteous; for the Lord knows the way of the righteous, but the way of the wicked will perish." Psalm 1:1-6 ESV

In high school, I was required to read and memorize Robert Frost's poignant poem "The Road Not Taken." Frost writes about two diverging roads in the journey of life and the choice that one must make.

Written centuries before Frost wrote his classic, the Book of David urges us to take the path that leads to a lifestyle that finds its foundation and source in our Creator. If we choose this path, we will find God's purpose for our lives that offers a joy and happiness that cannot be found in anyone or anywhere else.

Finding true happiness is a step-by-step, daily, and dynamic process that requires the personal discipline of reading, studying, and reflecting upon God's Word so that we can discern what God would have us do in each life situation or decision.

Before I accepted Christ into my heart, I had spent my first 40 years of life struggling with being in the will of God. I often chose the wrong path and falsely assumed there was no way of going back. However, God gave me the grace and wisdom to make a 180-degree turn that allowed me to start heading in the right direction. I learned that God's love and grace freed me to make the right choices, and these choices brought me happiness.

Similar to Frost's poem, David, through his words in Psalm 1, invites us to make a choice. While life's choices are oftentimes not simply black and white, the Psalmist says there are clearly two contrasting ways that offer two distinctly different consequences—"blessed" or "perish." These are found in the first and last words of Psalm 1.

Frost concluded his poem with these words, "Two roads diverged in a wood, and I took the one less traveled by. And that has made all the difference." Every day we are challenged with a new fork in the road of life. Sometimes the choice is not clear. Will we choose God's way, which promises life, or will we choose to go our own way?

I suspect that every day you face a new fork in the road. Maybe it is a decision to reenlist or leave the service. Perhaps it is a decision to get married. Or maybe you are thinking about going to school, selecting a new duty station, or maybe changing your occupational specialty.

When you reach the fork in the road, you can respond like Baseball Hall of Famer Yogi Berra suggests, "Just take it," or you can ask God to help you discern the path He wants you to take.

ENGAGE

As you look at the decisions in front of you,
ask God to help you make the right call,
to take the right fork that will help you
be the person He designed you to be.

DAY 20

Enough

"Go your way, eat the fat, drink the sweet, and send portions to those for whom nothing is prepared; for this day is holy to our Lord. Do not sorrow, for the joy of the Lord is your strength." Nehemiah 8:10 NKJV

In the movie *The Greatest Showman*, actor Hugh Jackman plays P.T. Barnum, an entrepreneur who's striving for acceptance and fame. Barnum creates a highly successful museum where the public can see live people with various physical abnormalities and eventually creates the highly successful Barnum and Bailey Circus.

He also contracts with Swedish opera singer Jenny Lind to sing on tour in the U.S. In the movie, Miss Lind, while on tour with Barnum, sings a powerful song titled "Never Enough." The song reflects Barnum's desire for more fame, riches, and, most importantly, acceptance by society's elite in spite of his already abundant notoriety and fortune.

I recently read about a stock trader, Sam Polk, who was obsessed with money. Sam shared in The New York Times in an article called "For The Love of Money" about his revelation that no amount of money was ever enough. He recounts that at the end of his first year on Wall Street, he was thrilled to receive a $40,000 bonus. For the first time in his life, he didn't have to balance his checkbook before withdrawing money.

Over the next few years, he worked like a maniac and climbed the ladder. Four years later, he was making $2 million a year, but was unhappy because everyone around him seemed to be making more than him. He later went to work for a hedge fund, and in his eighth year on Wall Street, his bonus was $3.6 million, but by that time, his greed had overtaken him. He was angry because it felt like even that amount wasn't enough.

Both Barnum and this stock trader could not find joy. While both men had more success and money than many of us could ever dream of, they desired more. Joy was elusive. Like Miss Lind's lyrics in the movie, whatever was achieved and possessed would never be enough.

King Solomon, in the Book of Ecclesiastes, observed that no earthly experience delivers ultimate joy and that no eye ever has enough of seeing, nor the ear its fill of hearing. Nehemiah writes that the prophet Ezra read the words of God's law to the people. The people stood in reverence for hours as God's Word was read, and as they began to understand it, they began weeping.

Ezra then told them they (and you and me) cannot conjure up this type of joy within ourselves, by our own power. It comes from only one source—the Lord. Thank goodness it's not our human joy, it's the joy of the Lord. Put another way, it's the joy God has.

Have you ever thought about the fact that God is happy because you have chosen to be in a relationship with Him? Knowing that God feels this way about you should spark the flame of joy within you, too! As believers in Christ, we have access to God's boundless joy—a joy that does not come from our circumstances, wealth, fame, acceptance from others, or within ourselves. It does not depend on how strong or even how spiritual we are. This joy comes from God alone and our personal relationships with Him.

The joy of the Lord is our strength. He is always, always enough for you and me.

ENGAGE

Please read Psalm 145. Think of the things you have that you can be thankful for. Write them down.

DAY 21

Limitations

"So God created human beings in his own image. In the image of God he created them; male and female he created them." Genesis 1:27 NLT

When our son Scott, his wife, Karin, and their family lived at West Point, Gail and I met their next-door neighbors, then-Captain Scotty Smiley, his bride, Tiffany, and their beautiful children.

In 2005, while leading his platoon in Mosul, Iraq, Scotty found himself in front of a suicide car bomber. As the man blew himself up, shrapnel blew through Scotty's eyes, leaving him blinded and temporarily paralyzed. As he lay helpless in the hospital, he resented the theft of his dreams, but with his wife's incredible love and the support of family and friends, Scotty's response became God's transforming moment. Although at times he questioned his faith, Scotty made a decision to forgive and rebuild his life, not to allow his vision limitation to define him, and to continue to serve in the Army, becoming the first blind active-duty officer in our Army.

Since the moment he made the choice not to give up while laying in a hospital bed, he has climbed Mount Rainier, won an ESPY Award, surfed, skydived, become a dad, earned an MBA from Duke University, taught leadership at West Point, led a U.S. Army Warrior Transition Unit, won the prestigious MacArthur Leadership Award, authored the book *Hope Unseen*, and taught leadership at Gonzaga University. He retired from the Army in 2015 and currently serves as an inspirational speaker and investment banker. Tiffany is equally impressive as a wife, mom, and the Republican candidate for U.S. Senator in Washington.

Scotty's story reminds me that we all have limitations. The Bible is filled with examples of simple people God used for great things. They all understood what it meant to be limited. Moses felt limited by his ability to speak; Gideon felt limited by his station in life and by his 300 men; the disciples felt limited with the five loaves of bread and two fish.

Facing limitations is something I believe everyone at one time or another understands. It could be a parental or marital relationship that seems impossible to repair. It could be your prayer life or spiritual walk with God that seems to be bogged down. It could be that your efforts to win souls or teach others about

Christ are unfruitful. It could be your stewardship or financial progress never seems to happen. It could be a desire to do something for God that is really out of your comfort zone.

Scotty and Tiffany's inspiring story invites you and me to ask, "What does God see in us, regardless of our limits?" More than anything else, He sees Himself. In the Book of Genesis, God tells us He created us in His image. As God's glorious image bearers, when others see you and me, we should reflect Him.

The Apostle Paul writes to the church at Corinth and tells them (and us) that we are being transformed into his image. Similar to Scotty Smiley, we can conduct our lives by Christ's transforming power, offering our lives as an anthem to the glory of God.

ENGAGE

What are your limitations? Pray today to ask God to help you reflect Jesus in your actions, speech, and simply how you interact with and serve others. Ask Him to help and transform you into the person He created you to be.

DAY 22

Fear is a Liar

"I sought the Lord, and he answered me; he delivered me from all my fears. Those who look to him are radiant; their faces are never covered with shame. This poor man called, and the Lord heard him; he saved him out of all his troubles. The angel of the Lord encamps around those who fear him, and he delivers them." Psalm 34:4-7 NIV

One of the great lessons the COVID-19 pandemic demonstrated to us was how fear can rapidly infect us and affect our thoughts, relationships, and actions. The broad band of media and political pundits, who offer much hubris and little fact, have created firestorms of fear, which have immobilized individuals, caused animosity and anger towards previously good friends, and manifested a climate of mistrust and air of conspiracy toward our major social and governmental institutions. Once-trusted institutions now follow perhaps only one political train of thought and vehemently criticize the differing perspectives of the other political parties and leaders, which only exacerbates and intensifies this fear.

The back story of Psalm 34 is that King Saul is on a mission to kill David. King Saul sees David as a direct threat to his power and influence, and David, in essence, is running for his life. David's word choices in this psalm speak of his fears, words such as *hatred*, *troubles*, *crushed*, *brokenhearted*, *afflictions*, and *deceit*.

David also uses words to share his faith and trust in God, such as *refuge*, *delivers*, *hears*, *saves*, and *redeems*. David's words demonstrate several important lessons that can help us as we encounter fear and deepen our faith and trust in God.

David shares that we are to praise God for all He has done and to extol the Lord at all times. He urges us to seek God with our whole hearts. Finally, David challenges us to draw closer to God to experience Him and His transformational love.

God never promised to keep us from facing trials. However, He does promise that He will be near to the brokenhearted and save the crushed in spirit.

What is your fear today? Perhaps it is an upcoming mission and the fear of being wounded or killed? Maybe your spouse got a bad report from the doctor. Maybe it is the fear of not being on the upcoming promotion list. Or has your child been struggling in his behavior and you do not know what to do? Today I challenge you, in the face of your fears and uncertainties, whatever they may be, to respond like David: Praise God, seek Him, and draw closer to Him. He is our hope.

ENGAGE

Write down the fears and uncertainties you are facing today. As you read over your list, offer them one-by-one to God, asking for His wisdom and strength. Thank Him for being with you in the midst of the trials.

DAY 23

Recovery

"David recovered everything the Amalekites had taken . . . Nothing was missing: young or old, boy or girl, plunder or anything else they had taken. David brought everything back." 1 Samuel 30:18-19 NIV

When I was attending the U.S. Army War College, my lead professor was a retired Army Colonel. Dave was an incredible professor, leader, accomplished author, and friend. One morning he came into the college's cafeteria and looked like he was in a state of panic. He came over to me and told me he had somehow deleted nine chapters of his new biography on Winston Churchill.

A novice to technology, he somehow deleted instead of saving the chapters on his computer. He had some notes on paper but realized it would take two to three months for him to rewrite these chapters, and his publisher's hard deadline was only weeks away. He was distraught, to say the least.

I was also a tech novice but knew there were some really competent tech consultants, known as the "Gold Coats" (nicknamed because of their work uniform) at West Point who had helped me before with computer issues. I called the academy, spoke to the Gold Coats, and within several hours, they walked Dave and me (we prayed like crazy while they worked) through the successful recovery process.

In the Old Testament, King David once led his own recovery mission. David and his army discovered that their mortal enemy, the Amalekites, had raided and burned down their town of Ziklag, taking captive the wives and children of his soldiers. David and his men wept aloud until they were exhausted.

In their grief, his soldiers became so bitter and angry with David that they talked of stoning him, but David found strength in God, who gave him the wisdom to lead his men to recover everything that had been taken from them.

I suspect that for many of us, there have been times in our lives, perhaps during deployment, when we have faced spiritual attacks that have attempted to steal our hope. It might be a loss of a friend or family member, a job loss, a financial loss, or perhaps a lost opportunity.

These attacks can be subtle or grow to become full-on spiritual attacks that leave us exhausted, frustrated, hopeless, and bitter. Like David and my friend Dave, may we today find renewed strength in God. He will be with us in every challenge of life. He will help each of us find hope if we trust Him.

ENGAGE

Have life circumstances tried to steal your hope? Never doubt God's goodness; never doubt God's love. Read the story of Joseph in Genesis, starting in chapter 37. Even in the midst of terrible circumstances, God took care of Joseph. He will take care of you as well.

DAY 24

Rest

"Be still before the Lord and wait patiently for him; fret not yourself over the one who prospers in his way, over the man who carries out evil devices! Refrain from anger, and forsake wrath! Fret not yourself; it tends only to evil. For the evildoers shall be cut off, but those who rest in the Lord shall inherit the land. In just a little while, the wicked will be no more; though you look carefully at his place, he will not be there. But the meek shall inherit the land and delight themselves in abundant peace." Psalm 37:7-11 ESV

I suspect all of us have had issues in our lives that have kept us up at night. You might have worries about a financial decision, an upcoming appointment with your doctor, a conversation with your spouse, or a hard discussion with your child. Likewise, during the lead-up to these decisions and meetings, you have most likely received advice from many people on how to resolve these issues.

DAY 24

When I am seeking advice or offered unsolicited advice, one of the first questions I ask myself is, "Does this person know and have experience in what he or she is talking about? Is he or she an armchair expert, or do they have actual battle scars?" David tells us we are to take refuge and be still in the Lord, waiting patiently for Him.

David's advice takes on significance when you understand what he went through. David was anointed by the prophet Samuel to be king, yet his path to the throne wasn't a cakewalk. Following his victory over Goliath, David had a brief moment of peace and then became a fugitive and had to flee from King Saul. Saul hunted David for seven long years, wanting to kill him. David had repeated confrontations with evil, yet his heart was not filled with hatred toward his enemy or bitterness toward God. Instead of blaming God, he turned to Him as his refuge, his hiding place, and his strength. When David says to rest in the Lord, you know it comes from a man who had battle scars and learned to rest through personal turmoil and challenge.

To enter into this rest is really an act of will and volition. It isn't something God does for us; it's something we do as we refuse to let worry take our peace of mind. In essence, we decide to put our worries and our welfare in God's hands.

I remember Chaplain Guy Lindsey offered this question to several of the infantry commanders just before we went to fight in Iraq: "If you were adrift on a tiny life raft on a stormy ocean somewhere, and a boat came alongside you, and Jesus cried out, 'Come here! Take my hand and get in our boat,' would you hesitate?"

Chaplain Lindsey was telling my fellow warriors and me that it is necessary to take a step of faith to leave the refuge of worry and allow ourselves to be lifted into the place of His rest. Staying outside in the storm with no shelter makes absolutely no sense when you can enter the palace of the King and find rest.

ENGAGE

Do you have worries today? Do you have issues that keep you up at night? Write down Philippians 4:6, then read through it as many times as you can until it is committed to memory.

DAY 25

Success

"By this we know love, that he laid down his life for us, and we ought to lay down our lives for the brothers." 1 John 3:16 ESV

I spoke with an Army officer who recently retired after 22 years of service. He explained to me that he had set his goal to be a general officer. He shared his list of achievements, his myriad of challenging assignments in peace and war, and his awards and advanced promotions.

He believed he'd been on the "right track." He then shared that his mother-in-law had a debilitating, terminal health issue, and he knew his wife wanted to move closer to help her in the final years of her life. Instead of achieving his goal, he retired from the Army and moved his family to a small town in eastern Oregon to care for his mother-in-law. This officer looked at me, tears in his eyes, and in a somber, quiet voice, said, "I feel like a failure because I never became a general officer."

I shared that he was not a failure because he gave up something extremely important to him to help someone else. I asserted that when we set aside our hopes, dreams, and aspirations and instead care for others, we're acting like Jesus. He nodded that he understood what I said, but I was not sure he completely agreed with me.

The soldier's life is known for its discipline, structure, focus on personal responsibility and selfless service. Soldiers learn to prioritize their health and fitness, develop a strong work ethic, and maintain a high level of accountability to their fellow soldiers. They also must clearly understand and be cognizant that their mission success is crucial.

Over the years, I have learned that earthly success is much different from what success is in God's eyes. God values the compassion that moves us to help hurting people. He approves of decisions and actions that protect people and stand up for those who are ostracized, minimized, or neglected by our self-centered, myopic society.

Jesus sacrificed everything—security, a home, and social acceptance to come to Earth and share God's love to a society that desperately needs Him, then and today. As the Apostle John notes, He gave up His life to free us from sin and show us God's love.

With God as our helper, aligning our values with His and committing our lives to love Him and others are the most significant achievements we can hope to attain.

How do you define success for your life? Has the quest for success, wealth, recognition, or celebrity affected your life? Is it difficult for you to align your values with what matters to God?

ENGAGE

Today ask God to open your eyes and heart to teach you how to align your values with His. Ask Him to teach you to love others the way He loves you. Now go out and do it.

DAY 26

Two by Two

"And he called the twelve and began to send them out two by two, and gave them authority over the unclean spirits. He charged them to take nothing for their journey except a staff—no bread, no bag, no money in their belts— but to wear sandals and not put on two tunics. And he said to them, 'Whenever you enter a house, stay there until you depart from there. And if any place will not receive you and they will not listen to you, when you leave, shake off the dust that is on your feet as a testimony against them.' So they went out and proclaimed that people should repent. And they cast out many demons and anointed with oil many who were sick and healed them." Mark 6:7-13 ESV

In the Army, one of the crucial fundamentals an infantry soldier must learn is how to build a protective foxhole. Dimensions, design, and construction worthiness are critical to the soldier's protection from direct and indirect enemy fire. Likewise, wise leaders know each foxhole should be made and manned by at least two soldiers. This allows for increased observation along with expanded range and direction of their weapons, and it offers time for rest or sleep for one soldier while the other soldier remains vigilant. Two or more soldiers in one foxhole bring synergy.

Jesus moved about in Galilee, sharing the Good News about the Kingdom of God and demonstrating the presence of the Kingdom through numerous works of His power. He also decided it was time to send out his disciples to share in His mission. Jesus gave the disciples authority over demons, as well as the power to heal the sick. They were assigned the mission to share the Good News with its call to rejoice, recognize, and repent. Jesus sent his disciples out "two by two."

I imagined several things as I read the passage mentioned above. First, I tried to imagine how the disciples felt going out on their own, away from Jesus. I suspect many said, though perhaps not aloud, "Jesus, are you serious? Do I really have to go with Matthew, John, or Thomas? Might I ask You to please rethink the part about no food, no money, no clothing?"

Also, as I read this passage, I wondered why Jesus sent out the disciples in pairs, rather than individually. Wouldn't one disciple be able to cover much more ground and in less time? In effect, this cuts in half the number of towns in which the disciples' ministry could be happening simultaneously. Part of the answer might lie in the Jewish tradition of "two witnesses." The Old Testament stipulated that at least two witnesses were needed in order to convict someone of a crime; this legal requirement underscored the common sense idea that two witnesses are more reliable than one.

There may be another reason why Jesus sent out His disciples in pairs. He may have been thinking of the power of shared ministry, the added impact when two or more people work together toward a shared goal. Jesus knew what the importance of teamwork would be when He would no longer be physically present on Earth. In building a team of 12 Apostles, He made working together to build the Kingdom of God an essential element of the Christian faith.

Here are some thoughts for you to consider this week:

- Who are your colleagues in your life, work, and ministry?

- Are there places in your life where you feel alone in your effort to serve the Lord?

- Who might be available to share in this ministry with you? Have you asked them to partner together?

Today and until He calls us home to Heaven, Jesus calls you and me to share His Good News. Today you and I, with God as our helper, must foster this same sense of collaboration, belonging, community, and purpose as the 12 disciples did. Let's start moving!

ENGAGE

Write a list of your partners in work, life, and ministry. Next, list ways you can encourage, support, and have their backs. Lastly, remember to pray for them daily.

DAY 27

Trophies

"What things were gain to me, these I have counted loss for Christ." Philippians 3:7 KJV

Like most military families, we have been constantly on the move to various duty assignments in the U.S. and in faraway countries. Even after retiring, we moved numerous times. Gail and I calculated that we have moved 19 times in almost 47 years of marriage.

Before, during, and after each move, we always try to sort out items we never plan on using again and do one of four things with each item: ask the kids if they want it; try to sell it; give it to a local charity; and if all else fails, trash it. Gail sometimes accuses me of throwing away things I shouldn't have.

As we were moving into our home in Oregon last summer, we found several boxes of trophies and awards our three children had won in their years of athletic competition. We thought about all of the sweat, broken bones, cuts, scrapes, blisters, and tears that had gone into gaining those awards, but we were now ready to put them in the trash. They no longer had any value to the kids or us. It is often said that one man's trash is another man's treasure—not so with these metal and plastic designs. Collectively, we agreed these trophies had no value to any of us, and no one in their right mind would want them either. They were junk.

So it will be at the end of our lives—all our possessions and things we've spent a lifetime working for will be nothing but junk. A pastor friend used to remark that he never saw a U-Haul trailer attached to a hearse. Hopefully, before our last days, we will understand and be cognizant that the best things in life are not things but relationships.

We can keep a proper attitude about our possessions because we possess the infinite greatness of knowing Jesus. Knowing Jesus and having a personal relationship with Him is the greatest treasure we can have. Knowing and enjoying Jesus is the point of the Christian life. When we lose this essential truth, you and I are doomed to a life of forever chasing after the next dream. We will continually compare our lives, our possessions, and our things to those of others. We will consistently play the "if only" game: If only I owned _____. If only _____ loved me. If only I could _____. If only I lived in _____. If only . . .

God wants a relationship with you and me. He wants to help you and me with everything we are going through and help us grow into the people He designed us to be. All that He asks is that we walk with Him, that we seek His will, and that we let Him into our hearts and lives. If you have not let Him into your heart, what is holding you back? Open your heart today and tell Him you are His. Because you are.

ENGAGE

Share this message with a family member, a friend, a co-worker, or a neighbor today. Call, FaceTime, or Zoom with them and discuss the gift that God offers us that will never lose value—salvation. With God as your helper, you just might lead another person to Jesus!

DAY 28

Wisdom

"Joyful is the person who finds wisdom, the one who gains understanding." Proverbs 3:13 NLT

Have you ever had a mentor, coach, friend, or family member whom you found to be wise and whom you always asked for his or her advice? My Army mentor, retired General David Bramlett, was such a person in my life. We first met when I was a Captain in the 101st Airborne Division (Air Assault). Four years later, we served together in the 101st again, and then years later, we both served at the U.S. Military Academy at West Point. David's vast leadership experiences in both peace and war and his expertise and scholarship in history have afforded me excellent counsel on a variety of leadership and people skills that have helped me throughout many roles and responsibilities.

I will never forget his counsel on working hard and doing your best: "Do not discount the influence of one soldier's commitment upon another, especially upon his leader. I have pushed myself harder in many aspects because of the commitment I see in the soldiers I have been privileged to lead. Their commitment is inspiring; they pushed me to my limits because I never wanted to let them down." Imagine that—a general who never wanted to let a private, a sergeant, or a young captain down.

The wisdom we choose to live by is foundational to our walk of faith. In essence, wisdom leads you to joy. The path to joy is paved with wisdom.

Solomon is noted throughout the Scriptures as a man of great wisdom. There are two crucial aspects that Solomon's life can teach us about wisdom. Solomon's wisdom was given to him by God in response to Solomon's prayer. This wisdom can be ignored, as Solomon clearly displayed when he turned from God to follow idols.

General Bramlett knows his wisdom comes from God. His humbleness and understanding that his wisdom is a gift is why I sought him when I needed counsel. His frequent admission that he does not have all the answers tells me he is very cognizant of and trusts in the One who does. His unpretentiousness reminds me of a Christmas card we once received that said, "Wise men still seek Him."

The wisdom of God will do incredible things for your life. When we ask for wisdom from God, it is with the understanding that what we are really asking for is for God to be glorified in our lives.

When you choose to ignore the wisdom of this world for His, the world will scoff and laugh, thinking you are weak, ignorant, or unwise. However, in asking God for direction, counsel, and wisdom, you will discover the path of living free. God's wisdom will lead you to a life that can only be found in Christ's grace, love, and mercy. Wise men and women still seek Him. How about you?

ENGAGE

Read James 1:5 today. God promises wisdom when we ask for it.

DAY 29

Trust and Humility

"Whoever wants to be my disciple must deny themselves and take up their cross daily and follow me." Luke 9:23 NIV

When Gail and I lived in Seattle, we saw the Blue Angels, the United States Navy Flight Demonstration Squadron, during Seattle's annual Sea Fair. The Blue Angels showcase the professionalism of the United States Navy and Marine Corps by inspiring a culture of excellence and service to country through flight demonstrations and community outreach.

During the demonstration, the fighter jets scream through the sky, flying in formations so close together that they appear to be just one aircraft. Every time these jets fly over, many in the audience wonder how they can fly so close together and not lose control. I met a former Blue Angel pilot and asked him this question. His response was three words: "Trust and humility."

Trusting that the lead pilot is traveling at precisely the correct speed and trajectory, the other wing pilots surrender any personal desire or inclination to switch directions or question their leader's path. Instead, they get in formation and closely follow. Trust and humility create an amazing team.

It's really no different for followers of Jesus. In speaking to His disciples, Jesus tells us that to be His disciple we must deny ourselves, take up our cross daily, and follow Him.

Jesus's path is obviously hard to follow as it is one of personal suffering and total self-denial. However, to be an effective disciple, you and I are invited to trust Jesus, put aside selfish desires, and begin humbly serving others first.

I once read that we should strive to live our lives in ways that others will see Jesus in how we act, speak, and show we care. By trusting in Jesus and humbly walking close to Him, we can appear as one with Christ. In essence, others won't see us—they'll simply see Him. Do others see Jesus in you through your words and actions?

ENGAGE

Pray today that you can trust God and humbly serve others as you live your life.

DAY 30

Waiting

"Wait for the Lord; be strong, and let your heart take courage; wait for the Lord!" Psalm 27:14 ESV

As professional soldiers, waiting seems like a standard operating procedure for us. We wait for our next order, we wait in the chow line, we wait for the aircraft, and we wait for the road to be cleared. We want what we want now—better yet, this instant! Standing in lines at the grocery store, waiting for an Amazon package to arrive, or for some, even waiting for the bread to be toasted can send us spinning.

While on a recent vacation, Gail and I waited close to 45 minutes to eat dinner at a restaurant that did not take reservations. While Gail was the picture of calm, I confess I did not wait well. Perhaps this is why God uses waiting to get our attention.

Waiting has been used by God many times in the Bible. Noah waited for the rain. Abraham and Sarah waited for the birth of their promised son, Isaac.

Joseph waited years in prison for a crime he didn't commit. Daniel waited through the night in a den full of lions. Paul waited in prison. Even Jesus waited 30 years before He began His ministry. If God even asked His Son to wait, what makes you think He would speed up the process for you and me?

While Noah waited for the rain, he began building an ark. As Daniel waited, he remained faithful in prayer and firm in his convictions. While Joseph waited in prison, he did his best with each responsibility given to him and stayed close to God. Paul and Jesus waited patiently and began the ministry God called each of them to do, caring for and leading the people around them.

In essence, there is always work to be done while we're waiting. Sometimes the work is hands-on, and other times it may be a solitary journey of prayer and fasting. Sometimes the work requires the discipline of patience; sometimes, it's simply about being present. When we choose to surrender to our waiting, when we believe our wait is part of God's larger story of our life, and when we embrace the physical and mental challenges of our waiting, the time we wait is never wasted.

The Lord, the Author of life and the Maker of time enters the journey of those who wait. As we continue to trust Him, He will reveal Himself to us along the way. Today, as you and I wait, allow God to show you where He is while we wait. Allow God to reveal to you and me what we can do to love and serve others as we wait.

ENGAGE

Write down the answer to these questions: How would you rate your waiting skills? What are you specifically waiting for to happen? Have you given your wait to God? Have you asked Him to reveal what we can do while we wait? What are you waiting for?

DAY 31

Hope in God

"But mark this: There will be terrible times in the last days. People will be lovers of themselves, lovers of money, boastful, proud, abusive, disobedient to their parents, ungrateful, unholy, without love, unforgiving, slanderous, without self-control, brutal, not lovers of the good, treacherous, rash, conceited, lovers of pleasure rather than lovers of God." 2 Timothy 3:1-4 NIV

Recent shootings and violence in many U.S. cities, both large and small, confirm that we live in very volatile times. Anger is ready to explode into physical violence at the slightest provocation. Our country seems brimming with hostility, anger, and violent acts that make no sense. Many times this violence is also very personal and close to home. It's in our neighborhoods, our schools, and where we work.

Home security systems and cameras are a necessity. Teachers and students are not safe in the classroom.

Store owners carry concealed weapons. Even churches lock their doors after service starts and have "greeters" who guard the doors to protect the congregation from a potential walk-in visitor who might intend to do harm. Centuries ago, in a dark prison, knowing his execution was near, the apostle Paul wrote his last words to his friend and coworker Timothy.

Paul's words have incredible relevance today. What do Christ-followers do in the face of violent acts that cannot be fully understood? We begin by turning to the One who fully understands. We go to God to express our outrage, concern, frustration, helplessness, pain, and vulnerability. God listens to us. God shares our outrage, concern, frustration, helplessness, pain, and vulnerability.

God will also whisper in His quiet voice. He tells us He is with us. God reminds us He loves us, the victims, and yes, even the perpetrator. God says to you and me, "I love you. I love those who lost their lives. I even love the person that brought this harm upon the innocent."

This is a part of our faith journey we often struggle with. I confess I do at times. We trust God for many things in our lives, but do we trust that ultimately God will redeem the situation? Do we really believe that God will make things right? Oftentimes we want to take justice into our own hands and deliver it in a fashion that matches the crime. But God asks us to drop our rights for revenge and trust Him to set things straight.

What good can we do in light of this current evil? What light can we shine into this darkness? I believe God is moving you and me to respond in a way that brings healing, peace, life, and hope for everyone involved. He will make things right. For He is God; we are not.

ENGAGE

Look in the mirror today and tell yourself you are not God. Then tell God He is your hope, and in Him you will trust. We know in our heads and hearts He will redeem the situations we face.

Final Thoughts

"Our days may come to seventy years, or eighty, if our strength endures; yet the best of them are but trouble and sorrow, for they quickly pass, and we fly away." Psalm 90:10 NIV

I was reading from a respected and credible online medical site that discussed suicide rates among soldiers and veterans. The study cited, "Multiple lines of evidence indicate that service in the military or after experience in combat and stressful situations has profound psychological and social effects. The psychological sequels of service in combat will probably persist for months and years to come."

Depression, isolation, loneliness, low self-esteem, sadness, and a feeling of hopelessness can cause a person to consider harming themselves. I recently spoke to an active-duty soldier who was contemplating suicide. He shared that his girlfriend had left him, he was arrested for a recent DUI, and the Army judicial system was determining if he should be allowed to stay in the Army. During one meeting, he remarked to me, "I really do not matter, Sir. If I die, no one would miss me; no one would care. I really do not matter."

Just consider for a moment what Moses said, "70 or 80 years if our strength endures." Our lives are so short. The brevity of life can cause us to wonder if we really matter. We're all searching for something in life. Whether you want to call it wealth, happiness, significance, purpose, meaning, or something else, there is an innate desire in each of us for our life to matter—to have significance and purpose.

The truth is that we are living significant lives simply because we have been made in the image of God. He is the one who gives us purpose. We matter because we're deeply loved by the God who made us. Moses later prayed and asked God to satisfy us in the morning with His unfailing love.

Moses' prayer connotes that you and I will rise to live and be loved forever. You and I matter because we matter to God. You and I matter because we can share God's Good News with others.

You and I matter because we can demonstrate God's love to others, leaving a legacy of God's love to everyone we meet on our journey. Life on earth is temporal. However, you and I were designed for eternity.

ENGAGE

Because of Jesus's resurrection and our faith in Him, we will live with Him in Eternity forever. You matter to God. Do you believe it? Please do, because it is true.

Acknowledgments

I wish to acknowledge and thank the following blessings in my life:

To my editors and literary coaches, Maryanna Young, Heather Goetter, Jodi Sherwood, and the creative team at Aloha Publishing for their love, caring, ideas, suggestions, and most importantly, their patience with my foibles.

To our three children, Scott, Jessie, and Meg and their amazing spouses, Karin, Luke, and Danny. You all are such a blessing in Gail's and my life.

To our eight incredible grandkids, Linnea, Caden, Celia, Eli, Lincoln, Violet, Estelle, and Tommy. "Gigi" and I could not be prouder of you. I am so fortunate to be your "Pap!"

To Gail, my best friend and wife for closing in on five decades together. I cannot imagine a better soul mate on this great adventure we have been on. You inspire me to be a better person every day.

And to Jesus for guiding me through the storms of my life and shining your light every day along my path.

About the Author

Colonel (Retired) Tom Greco served in the U.S. Army as an Infantry officer for over 24 years in peace and war. He is a West Point graduate and has a master's degree in business management from Central Michigan University. He is married to his best friend, Gail, an accomplished watercolor artist. They have been married for 47 years. Tom and Gail have three adult children and eight grandchildren. They live in Idaho, where Tom has served as the Civilian Aide to the Secretary of the Army for Idaho.

www.ingramcontent.com/pod-product-compliance
Lightning Source LLC
Chambersburg PA
CBHW022116040426
42450CB00006B/726